# Heartbreak And Coffee

Poems from a Patio

Tiffany Williams

BookLeaf Publishing

India | USA | UK

# Dedication

# Preface

There's an expression from one of my favorite philosophers that has stuck with me: The soul becomes dyed with the color of its thoughts.
I began writing this collection of poems from a patio in my backyard before a month-long wave of 99° days forced me back indoors. During this time indoors I found myself overthinking, self-reflecting, and self-loathing, which is easy for me to write about. It's not the most upbeat poetry you'll ever read but it's raw and honest. If you can deal with that, proceed. Thanks for stopping by.

# Acknowledgements

# Monsters Under the Bed

REMNANTS OF OUR PAST SHOW UP IN MY HOUSE
AND NO MATTER HOW I CLEAN I CAN'T GET YOU
OUT
REGRET UNPACKED IT'S THINGS
AND SAID HE'LL BE HERE TILL SPRING
I BRUSHED OFF YOUR COLOGNE, IT FELL AT MY
FEET
YOUR BREATH SETTLED IN LIKE DUST, NOW IT'S IN
MY SHEETS
YOUR LAUGH ROCKS ME TO SLEEP
I COUNT OUR DAYS LIKE SHEEP

THEN I HEAR THE MONSTERS THAT'S UNDER MY
BED
THEY WHISPER TO ME LIKE I'M ONE OF THEIR
FRIENDS
AND THEY ASK WHERE YOU'VE BEEN
I TELL 'EM I DON'T WANNA BE REMINDED

IT MIGHT BE MY EYES PLAYING TRICKS ON ME

BUT I SEE THAT YOU'VE MOVED ON AND IT'S
HAUNTING ME
AND YOU WON'T LEAVE
I KEEP TRYING BUT YOU WON'T LEAVE
ANOTHER DAY IS PASSING BY WITH A MEMORY
I WISH I COULD BLOCK IT OUT LIKE YOU DID WITH
ME
BUT YOU WON'T LEAVE
SO I KEEP CRYING 'CAUSE YOU WON'T LEAVE

SO I PACK UP ALL YOUR THINGS, THROW EM IN A
BAG
TILL YOUR TEARS FLOOD MY HOUSE AND IT BRINGS
EM BACK
THERE'S VOICEMAILS IN MY PHONE
THAT WON'T LEAVE ME ALONE

THEN I HEAR THE MONSTERS THAT'S UNDER MY
BED
'CAUSE THEY WHISPER TO ME LIKE I'M ONE OF
THEIR FRIENDS
AND THEY ASK WHERE YOU'VE BEEN
YOU'RE EVERYWHERE TO ME AND IT'S DRAINING

I THINK THAT IT'S MY EYES PLAYING TRICKS ON ME
BUT I SEE THAT YOU'VE MOVED ON AND IT'S
HAUNTING ME

AND YOU WON'T LEAVE
I KEEP TRYING BUT YOU WON'T LEAVE
ANOTHER DAY IS PASSING BY WITH A MEMORY
I WISH I COULD BLOCK IT OUT LIKE YOU DID WITH
ME
BUT YOU WON'T LEAVE
SO I KEEP CRYING 'CAUSE YOU WON'T LEAVE

I'M PRETTY SURE MY EYES ARE TRICKING ME
YOU SHOW UP ON MY COUCH WATCHING TV
AND YOU WON'T LEAVE
ANOTHER DAY IS PASSING BY, MEMORIES OF YOU
I WISH I COULD BLOCK IT OUT, BLOCK YOUR
NUMBER TOO
BUT YOU WON'T LEAVE
SO I KEEP CRYING 'CAUSE YOU WON'T LEAVE

# Lost and Forgotten Things

I'VE LOST MY LAUGH, HAS ANYONE SEEN IT?
MAYBE I SHOULD HANG POSTERS, OFFER A
REWARD
I'D GO TO THE ENDS OF THE EARTH, I MEAN IT
IF IT MEANT YOU'D WALK THROUGH THE DOOR

OR MAYBE I SHOULD VISIT THE PLACES IT USED TO
BE
SURELY SOMEONE THERE COULD BE OF USE
YES, I'LL GO TONIGHT WITHOUT DELAY!
YOU SEE, WHAT HAVE I GOT TO LOSE?

"IT SOUNDED LIKE THIS, YOU COULDN'T MISS IT,"
I DESPERATELY TOLD THE CLERK
"IT SLIPPED OUT ONE NIGHT, HAVEN'T SEEN IT
SINCE
I GUESS I GOT DISTRACTED WITH WORK."

JUST AS I SAID THAT HE SNAPPED HIS FINGER
AND SAID THAT HE'S SEEN IT AROUND

"MAYBE TWO YEARS AGO WITHOUT SO MUCH AS A
WHISPER
I CAUGHT THE OLD CHAP LEAVING TOWN
DON'T ASK ME WHERE, BY NOW IT'S LONG GONE."
I TIPPED MY HAT AND BID HIM ADIEU.
"I BETTER GET SOME SLEEP, IT'S NEARLY DAWN."
I PENSIVELY STROLLED DOWN THE AVENUE


BY NOW I'VE GOTTEN USED TO ITS ABSENCE
UNTIL A BLONDE-HAIRED MAN WITH A GINGER
BEARD
IN BETWEEN A SIP OF ABSINTHE
SAID, "THE THING YOU'RE LOOKING FOR IS OVER
HERE"
I STARED IN AMAZEMENT WITH A BRIMMING
SMILE
IT SOUNDED RATHER GUARDED AS IT SPOKE,
"HELLO, OLD FRIEND, IT'S BEEN AWHILE."
MY EYES SWELLED AND MY VOICE BROKE
I LOOKED AROUND TO THANK HIM BUT I GUESS HE
HAD OTHER PLANS
SO I PICKED UP MY LAUGH AND HEADED FOR
HOME
WHERE IT IMMEDIATELY DIED IN MY HANDS

# Debris

WHAT ENDED UP SO TRAGIC
STARTED LIKE ANY OTHER DAY
MUST BE SOME KIND OF MAGIC
YOU'RE TWO PLACES AT ONCE TODAY
OR DID I JUST IMAGINE
YOU AND HER ON JFK
YOU BLAMED ME FOR THE FALLOUT
AND I INSULTED YOU THROUGH TEARS
WHEN YOUR LOVE FINALLY BURNED OUT
IT LEFT LIKE IT WAS NEVER HERE
AND I JUST SAT THERE WATCHING AS IT ALL
DISAPPEARED

AND NOW I'M STUCK HERE
WITH THE GHOST OF YOU INSIDE THESE WALLS
THE TASTE OF TEARS AND ALCOHOL
I TOLD YOU SO'S AND WHAT-FOR'S
DEBRIS OF MY HEART ON THE FLOOR
DOES ANYBODY KNOW THE CURE?

I SET OUT ON A MISSION
TO WIPE THE PLACES WHERE I BLED
ALONG THE WAY I MISSED HIM
I COULDN'T CLEAN UP MY REGRETS
BUT I TRIED, I TRIED,I TRIED

AND NOW I'M STUCK HERE
WITH THE GHOST OF YOU INSIDE THESE WALLS
THE TASTE OF TEARS AND ALCOHOL
"I-TOLD-YOU-SO'S" AND "WHAT-FOR'S"
DEBRIS OF MY HEART ON THE FLOOR
DOES ANYBODY KNOW THE CURE?
THE TRACKS OF TEARDROPS ON MY FACE
THOSE TEXTS FROM YOU I CAN'T ERASE
I REPLAY TIMES WHERE I WENT WRONG
AND DROWN MY TEARS IN ALCOHOL
AND ON AND ON SINCE YOU'VE BEEN GONE

WHY DID I THINK BEING FRIENDS COULD WORK?
WE BUILT A LIFE AND THEN WATCHED IT BURN
AS I WATCHED YOU MOVE ONTO HER
UNLOCKED A FEAR I'VE NEVER KNOWN
WHERE IS MY CLOSURE?
I'M STUCK HERE TORTURED
WITH THE GHOST OF YOU INSIDE THESE WALLS
THE TASTE OF TEARS AND ALCOHOL
"I-TOLD-YOU-SO'S" AND "WHAT-FOR'S"

DEBRIS OF MY HEART ON THE FLOOR
DOES ANYBODY KNOW THE CURE?
ON AND ON AND ON AND ON
SINCE YOU'VE BEEN GONE
MAYBE I'LL ACT LIKE NOTHING'S WRONG
BUT I DON'T THINK THAT I'M THAT STRONG
LIKE YOU WERE WHEN YOU CARRIED ON

# Trying Times

ALTHOUGH I PUT THE DOGS TO SLEEP THESE
TIMES ARE TRYNA KILL ME SLOW
I THOUGHT I LOCKED UP ALL MY SKELETONS AND
LET THOSE DEMONS GO
BUT YOU KNOW, THERE'S CERTAIN SCARS YOU JUST
CAN'T COVER, I TRIED
IT SHOWS UP ON MY SKIN AND MAKES ME HATE
MYSELF SOMETIMES
NOW I CAN SHOW YOU STUPID PRIZES I GOT FROM
PLAYING IN THE HEAT
I'M LAYING IN THIS LONELY BED I MADE BUT STILL
CAN'T GO TO SLEEP
BECAUSE THE MORE I SIT AND THINK ABOUT IT
THE MORE IT MAKES ME MAD
NOW IT'S ALL ADDING UP BUT I WAS NEVER GOOD
AT MATH

NOW HE'S ON MY MIND EVERY TIME I GET A
TOOTHACHE
AND IT'S NOT A CRIME, I SAY AS I SELF MEDICATE

I'M HIDING IN MY CAR FAR FROM ALL THE
CRITICISM
DRIVING TO A BAR WITH NARCOTICS IN MY
SYSTEM
DON'T KEEP MIRRORS IN THE HOUSE, PICTURES IN
FRAMES
STUCK INSIDE A LABYRINTH OF ENDLESS SHAME
LEFT WITH NOTHING BUT WHAT'S COURSING
THROUGH MY VEINS
LEFT A BAD TASTE IN MY MOUTH AND ONE BAD
NAME

THOUGHT IF I STAYED ON THE STRAIGHT AND
NARROW I COULD BE REDEEMED
NO MORE ATTENTION WHORE
THIS GIRL'S NO LONGER RECKLESS AS SHE SEEMS
GO FIGURE
GUESS THEY WEREN'T KIDDING
THEY SAID, ENJOY IT WHILE IT LASTS
FORGOTTEN WHAT IT'S LIKE TO BREATHE
FORGOTTEN HOW TO LAUGH

CUZ HE'S ON MY MIND EVERY TIME I GET A
TOOTHACHE
AND IT'S NOT A CRIME, IT'S JUST LIKE MOTRIN FOR
A HEADACHE

VOICES IN MY HEAD ASKING ME, WHAT I WAS
THINKING?
HANGING BY A THREAD IN THIS PRISON I'VE BEEN
LIVING IN
DON'T KEEP MIRRORS IN THE HOUSE, PICTURES IN
FRAMES
STUCK INSIDE A LABYRINTH OF ENDLESS SHAME
LEFT WITH NOTHING BUT WHAT'S COURSING
THROUGH MY VEINS
LEFT A BAD TASTE IN MY MOUTH AND ONE BAD
NAME

LEFT WITH ONE BAD NAME
AND IT'S A CRYING SHAME
THIS GIRL WAS GOING PLACES
NOW SHE'S JADED

'CAUSE HE'S ON HER MIND EVERY TIME SHE GETS A
TOOTHACHE
AND IT'S NOT A CRIME, AT LEAST SHE'S TELLING
HERSELF THESE DAYS
TRYING TO FEEL NUMB AND OUTRUN ALL HER BAD
DECISIONS
POISON IN HER BLOOD AND NARCOTICS IN HER
SYSTEM
DON'T KEEP MIRRORS IN THE HOUSE, PICTURES IN
FRAMES

STUCK INSIDE A LABYRINTH OF ENDLESS SHAME
LEFT WITH NOTHING BUT WHAT'S COURSING
THROUGH HER VEINS
LEFT A BAD TASTE IN HER MOUTH AND ONE BAD
NAME, ONE BAD NAME

# Reflection

I'M FRIGHTENED OF MY MIRROR
CAN'T HIDE FROM THE FEAR
NO ONE KNOWS ME LIKE SHE DOES
"CAN'T YOU SEE THAT YOU'RE PRETTY?
DON'T LET HIM CALL YOU B**CHY
TIME'S UP, LET'S MOVE ON, IT'S HIS LOSS."


I FEEL YOU ALTHOUGH YOU'RE NOT HERE AT ALL
LIKE WAKING UP AND ALL YOUR TEETH ARE GONE


YOU CALLED ME FOREVER NOW YOU ACT LIKE I'M
DEAD
YOU SAID YOU COULD DO BETTER, THAT THIS WAS
ALL PRETEND
AND I CAN'T STAND TO LOOK AT MY REFLECTION
SHE'S COLD AND INTROSPECTIVE THROUGH AND
THROUGH
WHEN I SEE THIS GIRL BLEEDING IT MAKES ME SEE
THE TRUTH
THEN I THINK OF YOU

I'M WALKING WITH MY HEAD DOWN
EYES CLOSED, TRYNA TUNE OUT HER
"DON'T CALL OR THOSE LINES WILL GET BLURRED"

I FEEL YOU ALTHOUGH YOU'RE NOT HERE AT ALL
I'M CHASING A BALLOON THAT WANDERED OFF

YOU CALLED ME FOREVER, NOW YOU ACT LIKE I'M
DEAD
YOU SAID YOU COULD DO BETTER, THAT THIS WAS
ALL PRETEND
AND I CAN'T STAND TO LOOK AT MY REFLECTION
SHE'S COLD AND INTROSPECTIVE THROUGH AND
THROUGH
WHEN I SEE THIS GIRL BLEEDING IT MAKES ME SEE
THE TRUTH
THEN I THINK OF YOU

I'M FRIGHTENED OF MY MIRROR
CAN'T HIDE FROM THE FEAR
NO ONE KNOWS ME LIKE SHE DOES

# I'm the Problem

I GUESS I STILL EXPECT TO BE THE ONE YOU CALL
FIRST
WE SHOULD PROBABLY LOSE TOUCH
THE WAY THESE THINGS WORK
WAS I NOT GOOD ENOUGH WHEN YOU FELL OUT
OF LOVE
YOU FELL OUT OF LOVE

USED TO THINK THAT I WAS PRETTY
I USED TO BE FUN
PEOPLE USED TO CHASE ME NOW ALL I DO IS RUN
SICK OF FEELING GUILTY
MOST DAYS I FEEL FILTHY
EVERYTHING BUT NUMB

HOW DID YOU MOVE ON FROM THE STORM
WHEN THE WHOLE WORLD CRUMBLED AT MY FEET
YOU MIGHT THINK YOU'RE DOING ME A FAVOR
SHOWING ME HOW EASY MOVING ON CAN BE
I THOUGHT THAT WE COULD FIX IT

IF ONLY YOU WOULD LISTEN
MAYBE IT WAS ME
MAYBE I'M THE PROBLEM
MAYBE THAT'S WHY YOU'RE DONE
MAYBE IT WAS ME

I THINK WE ONLY GET ALONG WHEN I DON'T NEED
YOU
BUT THAT WAS ONLY FOR A MONTH, WISH I
COULD BE YOU
'CAUSE LATELY IT'S BEEN HARDER TO CONTROL MY
THOUGHTS
'CAUSE YOU'RE ONLY GETTING BETTER NOW THAT
WE DON'T TALK

USED TO THINK THAT I WAS PRETTY
I USED TO BE FUN
GOD, I HAD A LAUGH
NOW I DON'T FEEL ENOUGH
ALL I FEEL IS SH**TY
THIS DRINK HAS GOT ME DIZZY
EVERYTHING BUT NUMB

HOW DO I MOVE ON FROM THE STORM
WHEN THE WHOLE WORLD CRUMBLED AT MY FEET
YOU MIGHT THINK YOU'RE DOING ME A FAVOR
SHOWING ME HOW FAST FORGETTING US CAN BE

I THOUGHT THAT WE COULD FIX IT
IF ONLY YOU WOULD LISTEN
MAYBE IT WAS ME
MAYBE I'M THE PROBLEM
MAYBE THAT'S WHY YOU'RE DONE
MAYBE IT WAS ME


NEVER KNEW WHAT THIS LOVE THING COULD DO
TO ME
NEVER KNEW WHAT THIS LOVE THING COULD
MAKE OF ME
NEVER KNEW WHAT THIS LOVE THING COULD DO
TO ME
WHAT IT MADE OF ME, WHAT IT MADE


USED TO THINK THAT I WAS PRETTY
I USED TO BE FUN
I IGNORED YOUR PHONE CALLS
THEN YOU CALLED MY BLUFF
MY MIND IS SO CHAOTIC
NOWADAYS I'M TOXIC
EVERYTHING BUT NUMB


HOW DO I MOVE ON FROM THE STORM
WHEN THE WHOLE WORLD CRUMBLED AT MY FEET
YOU MIGHT THINK YOU'RE DOING ME A FAVOR
SHOWING ME HOW EASY MOVING ON CAN BE

I THOUGHT THAT WE COULD FIX IT
IF ONLY YOU WOULD LISTEN
MAYBE IT WAS ME
MAYBE I'M THE PROBLEM
MAYBE THAT'S WHY YOU'RE DONE
MAYBE IT WAS ME
I FEEL BAD FOR YOU

NEVER KNEW WHAT THIS LOVE THING COULD DO
TO ME
NEVER KNEW WHAT THIS LOVE THING COULD
MAKE OF ME
NEVER KNEW WHAT THIS LOVE THING COULD DO
TO ME
WHAT IT MADE OF ME, WHAT IT MADE
I CAN BE SO TOXIC

# I Never Think About You

HERE WE GO WITH THIS BS
I TRY MY BEST TO STAND ON MY FEET
BUT I DON'T KNOW IF I CAN
I SHOULD BE USED TO THIS RUSH OF SADNESS
THAT'S TAKING OVER MY PEACE
BUT I DON'T KNOW IF I AM
IT'S BACK AGAIN
CAN'T CATCH MY BREATH
I THOUGHT I TURNED A CORNER
BUT MAYBE I MISUNDERSTOOD
YOU MADE ME UPSET AND I BET
THAT NONE OF THIS IS TORTURE
GUESS YOU WERE HOLDING OUT FOR SOMETHING
GOOD

SOMETIMES I SEE THE SILVER LINING BUT RIGHT
NOW I LOST IT
I WANT TO START OVER BUT I'M TOO EXHAUSTED
I WISH THAT IN LIFE LOVE IS SOMETHING WE
CHOOSE

SO I DON'T HAVE TO KEEP PRETENDING THAT I
NEVER THINK ABOUT YOU

THERE'S NOTHING I COULD GIVE TO YOU THAT
YOU ALREADY HAVEN'T TAKEN
MY WHOLE LIFE'S IN YOUR HANDS
NOW THAT YOU'RE BUSY I JUST STARE AT THE
PHONE MAKING MYSELF DIZZY
I WANNA CALL BUT I CAN'T

SOMETIMES I SEE THE SILVER LINING BUT RIGHT
NOW I LOST IT
I WANT TO START OVER BUT I'M TOO EXHAUSTED
I WISH THAT IN LIFE LOVE IS SOMETHING WE
CHOOSE
SO I DON'T HAVE TO KEEP PRETENDING THAT I
NEVER THINK ABOUT YOU

AND I COULD TELL MYSELF I'M BETTER OFF ALONE
THAT I COULD GET USED TO THIS NEW LOW

SOMETIMES I SEE THE SILVER LINING BUT RIGHT
NOW I LOST IT
I WANT TO START OVER BUT I'M TOO EXHAUSTED
I WISH THAT IN LIFE LOVE IS SOMETHING WE
CHOOSE

SO I DON'T HAVE TO KEEP PRETENDING THAT I
NEVER THINK ABOUT YOU

21

# Snow Day

I WISH I WAS THE SNOWFLAKE THAT YOU CAUGHT
ON YOUR TONGUE
I KNOW WHY YOU HESITATE BUT I WANT TO BE
THE FIRST ONE
YOU CALL UP WHEN IT'S COLD OUT
AND I'LL BE READY WITH MITTENS IN MY
BACKPACK
I'LL KEEP MITTENS IN MY BACKPACK
I WISH I WAS THE SNOWFLAKE CAUGHT ON YOUR
TONGUE
OH I WOULD MELT IF I COULD I TOUCH YOU
I CAN ALREADY SEE THE REGRET ON THE HORIZON
WHAT AM I GONNA DO

SINCE WHEN DO MY CHEEKS START TO BLUSH?
WHEN DID ALL MY POETRY BECOME ABOUT LOVE?
I DON'T KNOW WHAT IS WORSE
I DON'T WANT TO FEEL NUMB BUT DON'T WANT
TO FEEL THE HURT
SINCE WHEN DO I FEEL INSECURE?

WHY DO I KEEP GOING BACK, WHAT IS THE
ALLURE?
THIS SLED'S GONNA CRASH AND BURN
BUT I STILL CAN'T GET OFF, THIS IS GONNA MAKE
ME LEARN

IT'S NOT A BIG DEAL
I KEEP SAYING IT'S NOT A BIG DEAL
IF I TELL MYSELF ENOUGH
I CAN STOP WHEN I WANT
IT'S NOT A BIG DEAL
I KEEP SAYING IT'S NOT A BIG DEAL
IF I'M HONEST WITH MYSELF
IT'S NOT GOING TOO WELL

# Demons

QUITE THE FREAK SHOW I WAS PART OF TIL I
FINALLY BROKE FREE
FIGHTING DEMONS JUST TO SEE THAT YOU HAD
PUT THEM THERE FOR ME
LOOK WHAT YOU STARTED
GUESS THAT'S WHAT YOU GET WITH CON-ARTISTS
AND WHEN IT CAME TO TAKING BLAME, WELL,
YOU WERE NOWHERE TO BE FOUND
YOU LOCKED US UP INSIDE THE HOUSE SHE BUILT
THEN BURNED IT TO THE GROUND
AND WHEN WE ARGUED
YOU SAID IT'S MY FAULT, THE NERVE OF YOU

COMPARED TO YOU AND YOUR RAGE MY DEMONS
SHUDDER AND HIDE
HAD I NOT TAKEN THE BAIT I COULD'VE TURNED
OUT ALRIGHT
I TRY MY BEST TO BE STRONG BUT YOU WAITED TIL
I WAS WEAK

SO YOU COULD STRING ME ALONG AND THEN
TWIST YOUR KNIFE INTO ME
WHAT A BACKSTABBER
IT'S A MASSACRE
LIKE WALKING IN A WARZONE EVERY TIME I COME
HOME

AND UP THE STAIRS I HEARD THE WHISPERS,
PEOPLE TRYNA BADMOUTH YOU
I GOT DEFENSIVE, SAID, YOU GOTTA LEARN TO SEE
HIS POINT OF VIEW
LIKE I WAS BRAINWASHED
I COULDN'T SEE THROUGH ALL THE CHAOS
WHAT WAS THE COST, WHAT WAS THE COST,
WHAT WAS THE COST
IF ONLY I HAD SEEN IT SOONER WOULD I PACK MY
THINGS AND RUN
'CAUSE YOU WOULD SHUT ME OUT AND PLAY THE
SILENT GAME LIKE IT WAS FUN
NOT MY FAULT YOU FEEL BURNED
YOU'RE STANDING IN THE HELL THAT YOU EARNED

COMPARED TO YOU AND YOUR RAGE MY DEMONS
SHUDDER AND HIDE
HAD I NOT TAKEN THE BAIT I COULD'VE TURNED
OUT ALRIGHT

I TRY MY BEST TO BE STRONG BUT YOU WAITED
TILL I WAS WEAK
SO YOU COULD STRING ME ALONG AND THEN
TWIST YOUR KNIFE INTO ME
WHAT A BACKSTABBER
IT'S A MASSACRE
LIKE WALKING IN A WARZONE EVERY TIME I COME
HOME

YOU TRIED TO BURY HER THEN TRIED TO PREY ON
ME
YOU TRIED EVERYTHING TO MAKE SURE WE COULD
NEVER LEAVE
YOU THOUGHT WHAT WORKED ON HER JUST
MIGHT WORK ON ME
OH WHAT A TWIST OF FATE, YOU
UNDERESTIMATED ME

COMPARED TO YOU AND YOUR RAGE MY DEMONS
SHUDDER AND HIDE
HAD YOU JUST SHOWN SOME RESTRAINT I
COULD'VE TURNED OUT ALRIGHT
I TRY MY BEST TO BE STRONG BUT YOU WAITED
TILL I WAS WEAK
INSTEAD OF PROVING ME WRONG YOU TWISTED
YOUR KNIFE INTO ME
WHAT A BACKSTABBER

IT'S A MASSACRE
LIKE WALKING IN A WARZONE EVERY TIME I COME
HOME

# You Deserve Better

I DON'T MEAN TO BE LIKE THIS
BUT I HAVE SOME BAD HABITS
MY TEMPER FLARED LAST TIME WE TALKED
YOU HAVE A SMOKE AND GO COOL OFF
WHEN IS IT OVER?
I CAN'T BELIEVE THE THINGS I SAID
OUR FRIENDSHIP'S HANGING BY A THREAD
I BLAME YOU FOR MY CUTS AND WOUNDS
IF I WERE YOU I'D HATE ME, TOO
WHEN IS IT OVER?

I DID SOME THINGS THAT I'M NOT PROUD OF
I ALWAYS HURT THE ONE I EVER TRULY LOVED
SO I'M DONE BEING AT WAR
BUT I'VE SAID THAT TWENTY TIMES BEFORE
I DID SOME THINGS THAT YOU DON'T DESERVE
I ALWAYS HURT THE ONE WHO LOVED ME AT MY
WORST
I KEEP PUTTING YOU THROUGH HELL
AND I ONLY THINK ABOUT MYSELF

SO WHEN'S IT GONNA END?
CAN YOU JUST EXPLODE?
WHEN'S IT GONNA END?
WHEN WILL YOU WALK AWAY FOR GOOD?
I DON'T WANT YOU TO LEAVE
BUT YOU DESERVE MORE

I SEND A TEXT, THEN TWO THEN THREE
UNSENDING MESSAGES WHILE YOU SLEEP
ABOUT HOW SORRY I SWEAR I AM
WHEN MORNING COMES IT STARTS AGAIN
WHEN IS IT OVER

I DID SOME THINGS THAT I'M NOT PROUD OF
I ALWAYS HURT THE ONE I EVER TRULY LOVED
SO I'M DONE BEING AT WAR
BUT I'VE SAID THAT TWENTY TIMES BEFORE
I DID SOME THINGS THAT YOU DON'T DESERVE
I ALWAYS HURT THE ONE WHO LOVED ME AT MY
WORST
I KEEP PUTTING YOU THROUGH HELL
AND I ONLY THINK ABOUT MYSELF

SO WHEN'S IT GONNA END?
CAN YOU JUST EXPLODE?
WHEN'S IT GONNA END?

WHEN WILL YOU WALK AWAY FOR GOOD?
I DON'T WANT YOU TO LEAVE
BUT YOU DESERVE MORE

IF I PUSH YOU AWAY AND YOU DON'T COME BACK
I'LL SAY THAT YOU DON'T CARE
THE F*** IS UP WITH THAT?
THEN I'LL MAKE YOU THE BAD GUY
THE F***ING NERVE
CAN'T TAKE IF YOU DO IT TO ME SO I DO IT FIRST

# Ghost

THINK THE CURSE IS OFFICIALLY BROKEN
I'M FINALLY READY TO LEAVE MY HEART OPEN
THEN I TURN AROUND AND THERE'S SNOW ON
THE GROUND
LIKE THE TIME WE-
OH WAIT, LET'S REFOCUS
THE GUY AT THE STORE CALLED ME GORGEOUS
HE TRIED TO MAKE ME LAUGH ON PURPOSE
I SHOULD SAY, WHY NOT
BUT MY WORDS HAVE BEEN BLOCKED
BY REPRESSED FEELINGS I DIDN'T NOTICE

OH, WHAT'S THE DIFFERENCE
IF YOU'RE GONE BUT YOUR GHOST STILL VISITS
HAUNT ME LIKE AN APPARITION
YOU COME AROUND AND THEN JUST VANISH

YOU SAY I ALWAYS PLAY THE VICTIM
THAT I ALWAYS ASSUME WHAT I'M MISSING
BUT WHEN YOU ACT SNEAKY

YOU KNOW YOU DON'T LEAVE ME
MUCH CHOICE BUT TO TRUST INTUITION
I WISHED THAT YOU WERE DEAD IN OUR LAST
FIGHT
NOW I DON'T KNOW HOW TO LIVE MY LIFE

OH, WHAT'S THE DIFFERENCE
IF YOU'RE GONE BUT YOUR GHOST STILL VISITS
HAUNT ME LIKE AN APPARITION
YOU COME AROUND AND THEN JUST VANISH

OH, WHAT'S THE DIFFERENCE
IF YOU'RE GONE BUT YOU'RE HERE IN SPIRIT
LOCKED UP IN THIS HAUNTED MANSION
WHY CAN'T YOU JUST GO AND VANISH

ALL OF THIS BECAUSE I SAID I WISH YOU WERE
DEAD
NOW I CAN'T LIVE WITHOUT YOU, I JUST SIT HERE
IN DREAD
I GUESS I SHOULD BE GRATEFUL FOR ALL THE
PATIENCE AND CHANGING
AND ALL THE GAS MONEY HE'S SAVING

OH, WHAT'S THE USE IF YOU'RE GONE BUT WON'T
DISAPPEAR

I WRITE THESE SONGS 'CAUSE I KNOW YOU'LL
HEAR THEM
WHY CAN'T YOU JUST GO AND VANISH

# Ignore the Signs

YOU SAID YOU COULDN'T STAY LATE
'CAUSE YOU HAD A LENGTHY DRIVE
BUT YOU WENT TO YOUR FRIEND'S PLACE
WE BOTH KNOW YOU LIED
AM I ONLY HERE TO FILL A VOID
AM I TEMPORARY
I KNOW THAT I'M NOT YOUR FIRST CHOICE
THAT ONE LEFT IN JANUARY
HOW CAN I BE SURE THIS TIME
YOU WON'T GO AND CHANGE YOUR MIND?

I GUESS I'M NOT A BURDEN ANYMORE
GUESS I'M NOT A LIABILITY ROTTEN TO THE CORE
GUESS TURNING A BLIND EYE MADE ME BETTER
THAN BEFORE
I GUESS I'LL IGNORE ALL THE VOICES SCREAMING
IN MY HEAD
ALL THE RED FLAGS, FLASHBACKS, THINGS MY
MOMMA SAID

I SEE THE FLASHING LIGHTS BUT LOVING YOU IS
BLIND
I GUESS I'LL IGNORE THE SIGNS

SHOULD PROBABLY ASK MY THERAPIST
BUT I'LL DO WHAT I WANNA DO
I THOUGHT THAT I WAS DONE FOR GOOD
BUT HELL, I THOUGHT YOU WERE DONE, TOO
IT'S MY TENDENCY TO KEEP SCORE
THE TERMS WE LEFT ON WEREN'T IDEAL
I KNOW YOUR LOVE IS JUST A METAPHOR
BUT THE PAIN IT CAUSED WAS SO REAL

I GUESS I'M NOT A BURDEN ANYMORE
GUESS I'M NOT A LIABILITY ROTTEN TO THE CORE
GUESS TURNING A BLIND EYE MADE ME BETTER
THAN BEFORE
I GUESS I'LL IGNORE ALL THE VOICES SCREAMING
IN MY HEAD
ALL THE RED FLAGS, FLASHBACKS, THINGS MY
MOMMA SAID
I'M GUESSING THERE'LL BE TEARS BUT LOVING YOU
IS BLIND
I GUESS I'LL IGNORE THE SIGNS

SHOULD PROBABLY ASK MY THERAPIST
LOVING YOU IS SUCH A RISK

IS MY HEART JUST DESPERATE
IGNORING ALL THE OBVIOUS

UNTIL REGRET'S KNOCKING ON MY DOOR
UNTIL MY HIGH HOPES BREAK IN HALF AND HIT
THE FLOOR
REMEMBER WHEN YOU SAID I'M EASY TO IGNORE
JUST LIKE I IGNORED THE SIGNS AND LET YOU
HAVE YOUR WAY
LET YOU HAVE YOUR CAKE AND EAT IT TOO THEN
JUST WALK AWAY
THE VOICES IN MY HEAD ARE LOUDER THAN
BEFORE
ALL 'CAUSE I IGNORED THE SIGNS

# Stupid Prizes

I'M TOO PRETTY FOR THIS
I CALL YOU A PIECE OF S***
'CAUSE YOU FLIPPED THE SCRIPT
LIKE I'M THE ONLY ONE WHO CAUSED THIS
GOT TEARS ON MY SHOULDER
YOU RELUCTANTLY COME OVER
JUST WANNA GO BACK TO HOW WE WERE
BUT YOU FELT ATTACKED
SO YOU ARGUE BACK
I SAY, "YOU REALLY SUCK"
TO MYSELF AS I THINK BACK
EYES ARE SMEARED IN BLACK
HANG UP, CALL YOU BACK
I'M F'D UP LIKE THAT

WHAT IT'S WORTH I REALLY DID TRY
BUT YOU'RE THE FIRST GUY
I THOUGHT DOESN'T LIE
READ BETWEEN THE LINES
LIKE I'M SEEING SIGNS

PLAY GAMES
ALL THE WHILE I'M TERRIFIED

AND WHEN YOU'RE THRU
I'LL SAY I KNEW IT
ALL DUE TO MY ABANDONMENT ISSUES
DID YOUR PHONE REALLY DIE?
WHY ARE YOU SO QUIET?
VOICES INSIDE MY HEAD INTENSIFY
I GOT MYSELF IN THIS MESS
THE ONLY THING LEFT
IS A FINGER PUPPET IN A ROOM FULL OF REGRET

PLEASE LET ME FIX THIS SO I CAN SCREW IT UP
AGAIN
UNTIL YOU CAN'T EVEN BE MY FRIEND...

# Paper

YOU DISAPPEARED AGAIN AND I TOOK IT TO MY
HEAD
YOU SAID YOU'RE WITH YOUR FRIENDS BUT AM I
NOT ONE OF THEM?
BLINDSIDED BY YOUR WORDS AND BURIED BY
YOUR ACTIONS
I KEPT FALLING FOR YOU BUT I'M NOT SOMETHING
THAT YOU'RE CATCHING
NOW IT'S BEEN A COUPLE HOURS SINCE YOU
CALLED WITH ALL YOUR S***
YOU KNOW I TEND TO OVERTHINK WITH EVERY
INTERACTION
YOU SAID THAT IT'S ON ME
I CRY TOO EASILY
I'M NEGATIVE, CONTROLLING, AND YOU'RE JUST SO
TIRED OF ME

YOU DREW YOUR SWORD AND RAN
DIDN'T WANNA ARGUE
NOW I HAVE TO CHECK INSTAGRAM

TO SEE WHAT'S UP WITH YOU
YOU HAD TO TREAT ME LIKE LESS
TO GET ME OUT OF LOVE
AND EVEN THOUGH IT'S FOR THE BEST
IT'S TOUGH IT'S TOUGH IT'S TOUGH
TO WATCH YOU TURN INTO A STRANGER
TORN UP LIKE PAPER

THE NIGHTS I'VE BEEN UP PACING AND CUTTING
MY HAIR
FROM THE IMPACT OF YOUR WORDS 'CAUSE THEY
STILL LINGER IN THE AIR
OH YEAH, I KNOW I PLAYED A PART, YOU WON'T
LET ME FORGET IT
BUT WHEN IT COMES TO YOU I BET YOU DON'T
EVEN REGRET IT
SO HOW COULD I STITCH UP THE WOUNDS
YOU POKE AT EVERYDAY?
BY BITTERNESS I'M SO CONSUMED
AND IT WON'T GO AWAY
BUT THE LESS WE TALK THE HAPPIER YOU SEEM
DON'T YOU MISS ME LIKE I MISS YOU?
ARE YOU RIPPING AT THE SEAMS?

YOU DREW YOUR SWORD AND RAN
DIDN'T WANNA ARGUE
NOW I HAVE TO CHECK INSTAGRAM

TO SEE WHAT'S UP WITH YOU
YOU HAD TO TREAT ME LIKE LESS
TO GET ME OUT OF LOVE
AND EVEN THOUGH IT'S FOR THE BEST
IT'S TOUGH IT'S TOUGH IT'S TOUGH
TO WATCH YOU TURN INTO A STRANGER
I'M TORN UP LIKE PAPER

TO WATCH YOU TURN INTO A STRANGER
SOMETIMES THAT HURTS EVEN GREATER
THAN HATING YOU FOR THE HUNDREDTH TIME
WHEN I LOVE YOU TURNS INTO GOODBYE

YOU DREW YOUR SWORD AND RAN, DIDN'T
WANNA FIGHT
NOW I HAVE TO CHECK INSTAGRAM TO SEE YOU
EVERY NIGHT
YOU HAD TO PUT ME TO REST TO GET ME OUT OF
LOVE
I KNOW THAT THIS IS FOR THE BEST
BUT GOD, IS IT SO TOUGH TO WATCH YOU TURN
INTO A STRANGER
I FEEL TORN UP LIKE PAPER
CAN WE TALK ABOUT THIS LATER?

# The Book of You

I KNOW WE'RE THRU BUT CAN I STILL CALL?
SHOULD I NOT THINK OF YOU AT ALL?
I WISH YOU WELL BUT NOT TOO WELL
I HOPE YOU DON'T MOVE ON TILL I DO
MAYBE I'LL FIND SOMEONE JUST LIKE YOU
MAYBE I PLAY TOO MUCH ADELE

THE GOOD TIMES, THEY FADE OUT OF VIEW
AND YOU WILL KEEP ME LOCKED UP IN THE BOOK
OF YOU
I PRAY TO GOD OUR STORY ISN'T DONE
BUT IF I'M JUST A MEMORY, CAN I BE YOUR
FAVORITE ONE?

I STARTED SCHOOL TO DISTRACT MY THOUGHTS
THE ONLY THING THAT I WAS TAUGHT:
YOU GOTTA GO THROUGH IT TO GET OUT
AND ALL MY FRIENDS SAY NOT TO CALL YOU
TO MAKE MORE PLANS THAT DON'T INVOLVE YOU
BUT I HEAR YOUR VOICE IN EVERY SINGLE CROWD

THE TIMES WE SHARED WHEN I WAS THERE BESIDE
YOU
WILL STAY LOCKED UP WITH ME IN THE BOOK OF
YOU
THE LETTERS THAT I WROTE TO YOU ARE GONE
IF I'M JUST A MEMORY, CAN I BE YOUR FAVORITE
ONE?

I HAVE TO WATCH YOU INSIDE PICTURES THAT I
USED TO TAKE
I HAVEN'T FORGOT YOU
YOU'RE EVEN INSIDE THE COFFEE I TASTE
YOU SNUCK INSIDE MY POETRY
BETWEEN THE LINES AND IN MY DREAMS
AND ON THE RADIO CONSTANTLY

WELL, ALL THOSE TIMES WE SHARED WHEN I WAS
THERE BESIDE YOU
WILL STAY LOCKED UP WITH ME IN THE BOOK OF
YOU
I FELT MORE THAN I CAN POUR IN A SONG
IF I'M JUST A MEMORY, CAN I BE YOUR FAVORITE
ONE?

# What a Joke

I BET MY THERAPIST IS SICK AND TIRED OF YOUR
NAME
SHE ROLLS HER EYES AT ME 'CAUSE EVERY SESSION
SOUNDS THE SAME:
"I REALLY WISH THAT I COULD LET HIM GO AND
FINALLY MOVE ON"
BUT SINCE I CAN'T I GUESS I'LL WRITE ANOTHER
SONG FOR YOU
I REALLY WISH THAT ALL THESE PILLS I TAKE
COULD GET ME THROUGH
BUT I KEEP THINKING EVERY NIGHT ABOUT WHAT
WENT WRONG

I'LL BE IN HELL WHILE YOU'RE OUT HERE HAVING
THE BEST YEAR
HOW COULD I EXPECT YOU TO CARE?
I'M UNDER YOUR SPELL AND I DON'T THINK I'M
GONNA MAKE IT OUT HERE
I DON'T KNOW HOW MUCH I CAN BEAR
WEREN'T YOU THE ONE I GAVE AWAY?

HOW IS IT THAT YOUR HEART ISN'T BROKE?
I'LL BE SITTING IN HELL WITH A WINE
WHILE YOU'RE WELL AND FINE
THINKING, WHAT A JOKE

I'LL BE HERE ANOTHER DAY WITH YOUR NAME ON
MY LIPS
WHILE YOU'RE OUT THERE AT THE MOVIES WITH
SOME OTHER CHICK
BECAUSE OF YOU AND ALL OF THIS I'M MORE
TOXIC THAN WHEN WE MET
I BET MY THERAPIST NOW HATES YOU MORE THAN
I DO
ALTHOUGH I'M KEEPING HER IN BUSINESS SHE
DESPISED YOU
WHAT HAPPENED TO, "I LOVE YOU AND WANT YOU
AND CHOOSE YOU"
I BROKE DOWN WHEN WE BROKE UP AND NOW
I'VE GOT SOME ISSUES

I'LL BE IN HELL WHILE YOU'RE OUT HERE HAVING
THE BEST YEAR
HOW COULD I EXPECT YOU TO CARE?
I'M UNDER YOUR SPELL AND I DON'T THINK I'M
GONNA MAKE IT OUT HERE
I DON'T KNOW HOW MUCH I CAN BEAR
WEREN'T YOU THE ONE I GAVE AWAY?

HOW IS IT THAT YOUR HEART ISN'T BROKE?
I'LL BE SITTING IN HELL WITH A WINE
WHILE YOU'RE WELL AND FINE
THINKING, WHAT A JOKE

THEY'RE TELLING ME CHANGE MY ATTITUDE
REMEMBER THAT TIME WILL HEAL ALL WOUNDS
THEY'RE TELLING ME CHANGE MY ATTITUDE
I DIDN'T ASK FOR YOUR PLATITUDE
THEY'RE TELLING ME CHANGE MY ATTITUDE
TO REMEMBER THAT TIME WILL HEAL ALL
WOUNDS
THEY'RE TELLING ME CHANGE MY ATTITUDE
BUT YOU CAN KEEP YOUR F'ING PLATITUDE

I'LL BE IN HELL WHILE YOU'RE OUT HERE HAVING
THE BEST YEAR
HOW COULD I EXPECT YOU TO CARE
I'M UNDER YOUR SPELL AND I DON'T THINK THAT I
CAN BREAK IT STUCK HERE
GOD, IT REALLY DOESN'T SEEM FAIR
WEREN'T YOU THE ONE I GAVE AWAY?
HOW IS IT THAT YOUR HEART ISN'T BROKE?
I'LL BE SITTING IN HELL WITH A WINE
WHILE YOU'RE WELL AND FINE
THINKING, WHAT A JOKE

# I BET MY THERAPIST IS SICK AND TIRED OF YOUR NAME

47

# 17. fwb

I HAD PLANS TO SEE MY EX ON SATURDAY
LACED UP MY CORSET REAL NICE
BUT SOMETHING GOT IN THE WAY
NOT A BIG SURPRISE
WHAT DO I HAVE TO DO
TO GET YOUR ATTENTION BACK
MY LIP GLOSS MISSES YOU
I THINK I MIGHT BE TOO ATTACHED
I'M MORE FUN THAN YOUR AVERAGE DOLL
YOU CAN UNDRESS ME AS YOU LIKE
WITH MY CHOCOLATE LEGS SO LONG
YOU CAN COME HERE AND TAKE A BITE
CAN I GET YOU TO STAY THE NIGHT?
HALF MY LINGERIE IS ON THE FLOOR
MAYBE YOU CAN ADD A LITTLE MORE
WELL, I'M TRYING AND FAILING
TRYING AND FAILING TO LET GO OF YOU

# Seeing Red

BLIND TO THE TRUTH NOW I SEE IT ALL TOO WELL
KISS YOUR NECK AND IT TASTES LIKE COCO
CHANEL
A RED FLAG 'CAUSE I AIN'T WORN THAT SCENT IN
QUITE AWHILE
SEEING RED LIKE THE LIPSTICK ON YOUR CHEEK
I'M WIDE AWAKE WHILE BABY, YOU'RE SOUND
ASLEEP
I'M OUT OF BREATH 'CAUSE MY IMAGINATION'S
RUNNING WILD
THESE SCENARIOS I DREAD SWIRLING IN MY HEAD
COME TRUE
YOUR BODY'S HERE IN THIS HOTEL BUT SHE MIGHT
AS WELL BE, TOO

I CAN SEE HER RED DRESS IN YOUR BROWN EYES
WHEN OURS CONNECT
I CAN SEE THOSE RED SHOES WHEN I CATCH YOU
SMILING OUT OF THE BLUE
MAYBE I SHOULD BE WHAT YOU SEE IN HER

BABY, I COULD BE COLORFUL
I CAN GUESS WHAT HAPPENED
BUT I GET SO UPSET THAT IT'S ALL RED

YOU'RE UNDER MY SKIN SO I GET UNDRESSED
SLIDE MY PANTIES OFF AND KICK EM NEXT TO
YOUR HEAD
I WANNA GET YOUR MIND OFF HER AND ON ME
FOR AWHILE
I CAN FEEL HER IN THE ROOM AND SHE'S PULLING
YOU FROM ME
YOU MAY DENY THAT SHE EXISTS BUT YOUR
FINGERTIPS TELL ME

I CAN SEE HER RED DRESS IN YOUR BROWN EYES
WHEN OURS CONNECT
I CAN SEE THOSE RED SHOES WHEN I CATCH YOU
SMILING OUT OF THE BLUE
MAYBE I SHOULD BE WHAT YOU SEE IN HER
BABY I COULD COLORFUL
I CAN GUESS WHAT HAPPENED
BUT I GET SO UPSET THAT IT'S ALL RED

I GET SO UPSET THAT ALL I SEE IS RED
YOUR PHONE GOES OFF AT NIGHT
IT'S NOT WORTH THE FIGHT
WHEN YOU FANTASIZE

YOUR GUILTY EYES SAY WHAT'S IN YOUR HEAD
RED IS IN HER SMILE, FIERY AND WILD
IT'S IN THE POISON YOU DRINK THAT I THINK YOU
PREFER INSTEAD

I CAN SEE HER RED DRESS IN YOUR BROWN EYES
WHEN OURS CONNECT
I CAN SEE THOSE RED SHOES
IT'S LIKE SHE'S STANDING HERE IN THIS ROOM
MAYBE I SHOULD BE COLORFUL
BABY, I COULD BE MUCH BETTER
I CAN GUESS WHAT HAPPENED
BUT I GET SO UPSET THAT IT'S ALL RED

# 19. Bad Apologies

COULD'VE HANDLED IT BETTER BUT WHAT ABOUT
YOU
BRINGING UP OLD STUFF LIKE YOU ALWAYS DO
ALL OF THIS FIGHTING STARTED CUZ OF YOU
I'M SORRY I'M SORRY I'M SORRY YOU FEEL THAT
WAY

SOMETIMES YOU MAKE IT SO HARD WHEN YOU'RE
ALWAYS ACCUSING ME OF LYING
WHY DON'T YOU JUST TAKE A STEP BACK AND
RELAX BECAUSE I DON'T FEEL LIKE FIGHTING
YOU SAY YOU'RE HURT BUT THAT WAS NOT
INTENTION
I'LL BE THE BAD GUY, YOU'RE CLEARLY OFFENDED
WE COULD MOVE ON BUT YOU DON'T APPRECIATE
HONESTY
WELL I'M NOT A PRIEST SO F YOUR APOLOGY

YOU ALWAYS ASSUME THAT I'M CAUGHT IN A LIE

YOU DIG AND YOU DIG TILL YOU MAKE YOURSELF
CRY
I'D RATHER KEEP SECRETS INSTEAD OF EXPLAIN
BUT THEN YOU TURN AROUND AND COMPLAIN
GOT ME FEELING SO DRAINED
GUESS I'LL JUST CALL YOU WHEN YOU'RE FINISHED
TRIPPING


YOU SAY YOU'RE HURT BUT THAT WAS NOT MY
INTENTION
I'LL BE THE BAD GUY, YOU'RE CLEARLY OFFENDED
WE COULD MOVE ON BUT YOU DON'T APPRECIATE
HONESTY
WELL, I'M NOT A PRIEST SO F YOUR APOLOGY
WELL, I'M NOT A PRIEST SO F YOUR APOLOGY
WELL, I'M NOT A PRIEST SO F YOUR APOLOGY


SOMETIMES YOU MAKE IT SO HARD WHEN YOU'RE
ALWAYS ACCUSING ME OF LYING
WHY DON'T YOU JUST TAKE A STEP BACK AND
RELAX BECAUSE I DON'T FEEL LIKE FIGHTING
YOU SAY YOU'RE HURT BUT THAT WAS NOT MY
INTENTION
I'LL BE THE SCAPEGOAT IF YOU'RE OFFENDED
YOU THROW A FIT BECAUSE YOU CAN'T HANDLE
HONESTY
WELL, I'M NOT A PRIEST SO F YOUR APOLOGY

WELL, I'M NOT A PRIEST SO F YOUR APOLOGY
WELL, I'M NOT A PRIEST SO KEEP YOUR APOLOGY

# 20. Falling for Boys

I'M SO SICK AND TIRED OF FALLING FOR WHAT
PASSES AS A COMPLIMENT
WOULD RATHER HAVE SOME COMMON SENSE
LOOK AT ME IGNORING ALL THE RED FLAGS
ANOTHER YEAR THAT I CAN'T GET BACK
I SAY I'M SO DONE WITH MAKING UP EXCUSES
BUT THEN THERE GOES ANOTHER ONE
YOU'D THINK THAT I WAS HAVING FUN
THE WAY THAT I'M IGNORING ALL THE RED FLAGS
ANOTHER YEAR THAT I CAN'T GET BACK

WHAT I REALLY WANT IS MY SPIRIT BACK
NOT GETTING STABBED IN THE BACK
HOPING YOU'LL CHANGE
WHAT I REALLY WANT IS MY SPIRIT BACK
NOT TO GET STABBED IN THE BACK
MISSING MY LAUGH

BUT WHAT CAN I SAY
I ATTRACT GUYS WHO DON'T APOLOGIZE

WHO KEEP ME UP AT NIGHT TO TELL ME SWEET
LITTLE LIES
KEEP ME A SECRET FROM THEIR FAMILY AND
FRIENDS
I KEEP FALLING FOR BOYS AND MISTAKING THEM
FOR MEN

THE ONES WITH A RECORD, HIDING AND
SCHEMING
PEOPLE NAMED SHAWN WHO BLAME YOU FOR
CHEATING
IT MUST BE THE TATTOOS
LOOK WHAT I GOT MYSELF INTO
THEY DON'T WANNA FIGHT THEN PROCEED TO
ARGUE
PEOPLE NAMED JON WHO LIE THAT THEY LOVE
YOU
WEIRD MOMMY ISSUES
LOOK WHAT I GOT MYSELF INTO

WHAT I REALLY WANT IS MY SPIRIT BACK
NOT TO GET STABBED IN THE BACK
HOPING YOU'LL CHANGE
WHAT I REALLY WANT IS MY SPIRIT BACK
NOT TO GET STABBED IN THE BACK
MISSING MY LAUGH

BUT WHAT CAN I SAY
I ATTRACT GUYS WHO DON'T APOLOGIZE
WHO KEEP ME UP LATE TO TELL ME SWEET LITTLE
LIES
KEEP ME A SECRET FROM THEIR FAMILY AND
FRIENDS
I KEEP FALLING FOR BOYS AND MISTAKING THEM
FOR MEN

I'M SO SICK AND TIRED OF FALLING FOR WHAT
PASSES AS A COMPLIMENT
WOULD RATHER HAVE SOME COMMON SENSE
LOOK AT ME IGNORING ALL THE RED FLAGS
ANOTHER YEAR THAT I CAN'T GET BACK

# 21. Adam

I THINK THAT I'M A BIT CONFUSED BUT HONESTLY
I'M NOT THAT SURPRISED AND NEITHER IS HE
IT MIGHT BE THE RULES OR DADDY ISSUES
BUT I'VE GOT A FEELING THAT I MIGHT JUST GET
ATTACHED
TO ONE MORE GUY THAT I CAN NEVER HAVE
BUT I DO IT ANYWAY

OH MY TENDENCIES ARE DRIVING ME CRAZY
IT FEELS LIKE A DISEASE THAT I'M CATCHING YOU
QUICKLY
I'M SO SICK OF MYSELF
GOD, I WISH I WAS WELL
SOMEONE SEND HELP
'CAUSE SOMETHING'S GOT A HOLD ON ME
AND IT'S HOLDING ON WELL

NOW I THINK I'LL WATCH THE BRITISH VERSION OF
THE OFFICE
TO FEEL CLOSER TO YOU WITHOUT TAKING A RISK

AND WHEN THEY SAY TIFF, WHAT'S GOT YOU LIKE
THIS
IN MY HEAD I'LL SAY, MY THERAPIST
A TENDENCY HE KNOWS
TO FALL FOR GUYS WHO KEEP ME ON MY TOES
AND WHO PUSH ME AWAY

OH MY TENDENCIES ARE DRIVING ME CRAZY
IT FEELS LIKE A DISEASE THAT I'M CATCHING YOU
QUICKLY
I'M SO SICK OF MYSELF
GOD, I WISH I WAS WELL
SOMEONE SEND HELP
'CAUSE SOMETHING'S GOT A HOLD ON ME

I KNOW YOU DON'T THINK ABOUT ME AS YOU'RE
LIVING YOUR LIFE
WITH YOUR FANCY DEGREE AND YOUR BEAUTIFUL
WIFE
WITH ALL YOUR GINGER HAIR
A SENSE OF HUMOR, TOO
NO TIME TO LIST ALL THE THINGS THAT I LIKE
ABOUT YOU
BUT ALL YOU SEE WHEN YOU LOOK AT ME IS
IDIOSYNCRASIES
ALL YOU SEE WHEN YOU LOOK AT ME IS
IDIOSYNCRASIES

OH MY TENDENCIES ARE DRIVING ME CRAZY
IT ALWAYS SEEMS TO BE THE CAUSE OF YOUR
BOUNDARIES
I'M SO SICK OF THIS HELL
GOD I WISH I COULD BE WELL
SOMEONE SEND HELP
'CAUSE SOMETHING'S GOT A HOLD ON ME
AND IT'S HOLDING ON WELL